The Flavours Series

SUMMER VEGETABLES

ELAINE ELLIOT

Photography by Julian Beveridge

FORMAC PUBLISHING COMPANY LIMITED
HALIFAX 2000

PHOTO CREDITS:
All photographs by Julian Beveridge.

PARTICIPATING ESTABLISHMENTS:
Amherst Shore Country Inn, Lorneville, NS
Arbor View Inn, Lunenburg, NS
Blomidon Inn, Wolfville, NS
Candleriggs, Indian Point, NS
Catherine McKinnon's Spot O'Tea Restaurant,
    Stanley Bridge, PEI
Charlotte Lane Café and Crafts,
    Shelburne, NS
Duncreigan Country Inn, Mabou, NS
Dundee Arms, Charlottetown, PEI
Falcourt Inn, Nictaux, NS
Florentine Manor Heritage Inn, Albert, NB
Gowrie House Country Inn,
    Sydney Mines, NS

Halliburton House Inn, Halifax, NS
Innlet Café, Mahone Bay, NS
Inn on the Lake, Waverley, NS
Jubilee Cottage Country Inn, Wallace, NS
The Ledges Inn, Doaktown, NB
Little Shemogue Country Inn, Port Elgin, NB
Marshlands Inn, Sackville, NB
The Murray Manor Bed and Breakfast,
    Yarmouth, NS
Pete's Frootique, Bedford, NS
Seasons in Thyme, Summerside, PEI
Shadow Lawn Country Inn, Rothesay, NB
The Whitman Inn, Kempt, NS
The Windsor House of St. Andrews,
    St. Andrews, NB

This book is dedicated with love to my granddaughter Jessica Elliot of Nova Scotia and my grandson Cameron Elliot of New Brunswick.

Formac Publishing Company Limited acknowledges the support of the Cultural Affairs Section, Nova Scotia Department of Tourism and Culture. We acknowledge the financial support of the Government of Canada through the Book Publishing Industry Development Program (BPIDP) for our publishing activities.

Canadian Cataloguing in Publication Data

Elliot, Elaine, 1939–
        Summer Vegetables
        (Maritime Flavours)
        Includes index.
        ISBN 0-88780-508-6

1. Cookery (Vegetables) I. Title. II. Series.
TX801.E524 2000   641.6'5   C00-950010-3

Formac Publishing Company Limited
5502 Atlantic Street
Halifax, Nova Scotia
B3H 1G4

Distribution in the United States:
Seven Hills Book Distributors
1531 Tremont Street
Cincinnati, Ohio 45214

Printed in China

CONTENTS

INTRODUCTION

*B*lessed are the chefs who have a source of fresh summer vegetables and fragrant herbs close by their kitchen door! Freshly pulled carrots, tender baby zucchini, crisp yellow or green beans, plump tomatoes, ripened on the vine in the late summer sun are but a few of the ingredients used to prepare these memorable dishes. Alas, most cooks do not have the good fortune to have a kitchen garden, and must rely upon farm vegetable stands and greengrocers to provide fresh produce.

Most of the ingredients called for in these recipes feature locally grown summer produce rather than exotic imports. These vegetables are fresher than imported varieties, and you should choose the freshest produce available. Look for firm, full-coloured vegetables, and use as close to their harvest as possible. Crisp vegetables, such as lettuce, carrots, cauliflower, celery, cucumbers, and broccoli, should be stored in plastic bags in the crisper section and consumed within a few days. A few vegetables such as turnips, potatoes, and winter squash should not be refrigerated, but

stored in a cool, dark area which allows space for air to circulate. Tomatoes, which are in fact fruit, should be placed in a bowl and kept at room temperature until fully ripened. Care and storage of the various vegetables vary greatly, but remember, your produce manager is an expert in his or her field, so do not hesitate to ask questions about freshness, cooking techniques and storage.

This is the eleventh book in the Flavour Series and I again invited the chefs of Eastern Canada's acclaimed inns and restaurants to share their special vegetable recipes. Their contributions demonstrate their desire to use fresh local produce, but with a flair. Photographer Julian Beveridge has visited many of their dining rooms, capturing the dishes as they are served to guests. Each recipe has been tested and adjusted to serve four to six persons.

This book is an explosion of innovations in

fine cuisine. From Seasons in Thyme's Spring Asparagus Soup with Malpeque Oysters to the Blomidon Inn's famous Ratatouille, or Falcourt Inn's Wicked Whipped Squash, you will find an array of finger foods, appetizers, soups, salads, make-ahead vegetable dishes and entrée accompaniments. Be daring, study the pictorial presentations and serve a meal that is memorable. Bon appétit!

APPETIZERS

*W*ake up, taste buds, we are on a roll! From finger foods to more elegant starters, this section provides suggestions for delightful first-course fare.

◄ Tender green beans wrapped in Italian prosciutto as served at the Little Shemogue Country Inn

GREEN BEANS WITH PROSCIUTTO AND YOGHURT HERB DRESSING

LITTLE SHEMOGUE COUNTRY INN, PORT ELGIN, NB

Prosciutto is a salt-cured, air-dried, ready-to-eat ham that is sold in paper thin slices in the deli section of most large supermarkets. Owner-chef Petra Sudbrack of the Little Shemogue wraps fresh green beans with prosciutto making an impressive first-course dish.

2 eggs, hard boiled

1 small white onion, peeled and diced

1 cup plain yoghurt

1/3 cup egg-based mayonnaise

3 tablespoons finely chopped herbs, (dill, chives, parsley, etc.)

1 pound fresh green beans

1/2 teaspoon salt

2 tablespoons extra virgin olive oil

4 slices rye bread

freshly ground black pepper

1/4 pound prosciutto

Peel eggs and chop into a fine dice.

Peel and finely dice onion.

In a small bowl combine yoghurt, mayonnaise, chopped herbs, eggs, and onion. Refrigerate.

Rinse beans and blanch in boiling salted water until crisp tender, approximately 10 minutes. Drain and immediately immerse in ice water to stop the cooking process; thoroughly drain again.

Heat olive oil in a skillet over medium heat. Slice bread into 1-inch wide strips and saute in oil. Sprinkle with pepper and turn, to brown evenly.

To serve, divide beans into bundles, wrap with prosciutto and place on warm rye toast. Serve sauce on the side.

Serves 4.

GRILLED SUMMER SQUASH BAGUETTE

SHADOW LAWN COUNTRY INN, ROTHESAY, NB

Chef Glen White of Shadow Lawn Inn serves his baguette "sandwich-style," chock full of tender summer vegetables of contrasting colours.

2 each baby yellow and green zucchini

1 red bell pepper

Vegetable Marinade, recipe follows

2 tablespoons Pommery mustard

1 sour-dough baguette, sliced in half lengthwise

2 tablespoons pesto

1/2 cup salad greens

Vegetable Marinade

1 tablespoon chopped onion

1/2 cup soya sauce

1/4 cup extra virgin olive oil

1/4 cup rice wine vinegar

1 tablespoon chopped herbs (rosemary, thyme, basil, etc.)

salt and pepper, to taste

Slice zucchini into thin strips. Cut pepper into wedges. Toss vegetables in marinade and let stand 30 minutes.

Drain vegetables and grill until crisp tender.

Rub cut sides of baguette with pesto. Grill baguette to toast. Brush baguette with mustard and top with grilled vegetables. Slice and serve warm with salad greens as garnish.

Combine all ingredients in a bowl.

MUSHROOM SPREAD

MURRAY MANOR BED AND
BREAKFAST, YARMOUTH, NS

Innkeeper Joan Semple treats guests to a variety of refreshing appetizers. This spread is easy to prepare and may be served warm or chilled, on small crackers or in tiny pre-baked tart shells.

1/2 pound mushrooms

1 medium onion, finely chopped

2 tablespoons butter

1/2 teaspoon salt

pinch freshly ground black pepper

pinch ground nutmeg

1 teaspoon lemon juice

2 teaspoons flour

1/2 cup sour cream

1/2 to 1 teaspoon dried dill weed

Clean and trim mushrooms before chopping finely. Melt butter and sauté mushrooms and onions, stirring often for 4 minutes. Sprinkle with salt, pepper, nutmeg, lemon juice and flour. Continue to cook 1–2 minutes. Remove from heat and stir in sour cream and dill. Serve warm or chilled.

Serves 4–6.

BRUSCHETTA STEFAN STYLE

SEASONS IN THYME, SUMMERSIDE, PEI

Prepare this bruschetta when vine-ripened tomatoes are at their peak!

1 extra large tomato, peeled and diced

pinch salt

pinch sugar

1 teaspoon melfour vinegar*

1 teaspoon balsamic vinegar

1 tablespoon olive oil

1 teaspoon chopped basil (1/3 teaspoon dried)

1 garlic clove

slightly toasted baguette bread slices

Slice a cross across the stem end of tomato. Quickly blanch tomato in boiling water for half a minute, remove and immerse in cold water. Slip skin from tomato and dice. Combine tomato, salt, sugar, vinegars, olive oil and basil.

Lightly toast baguette slices then rub with garlic clove. Spoon a tablespoon of tomato mixture on toast slices.

Serves 4.

* If melfour vinegar is unavailable, substitute an equal amount of maple vinegar, or cider vinegar, plus 1 teaspoon liquid honey.

Bruschetta Stefan Style ▶

CHARLOTTE LANE FENNEL AND PEAR GRATIN

CHARLOTTE LANE CAFÉ AND CRAFTS, SHELBURNE, NS

Although this dish is featured in the appetizer section, chef Roland Glauser of Charlotte Lane advises that it is equally delicious served as an accompaniment to a meat or seafood entrée.

2 medium-sized fennel bulbs

water to cover

1/4 teaspoon salt

1/2 half fresh lemon, sliced

2 large pears

water to cover

4 teaspoons sugar

1 1/2 fresh lemon, sliced

1/2 cup beef broth

salt and pepper, to taste

2 ounces Parmesan cheese, coarsely grated

fresh basil sprigs, as garnish

Remove all stems from fennel and halve bulb. Simmer in salted water with half a lemon until soft, approximately 30–40 minutes. Remove from heat and drain.

Peel and core pears and simmer in water with sugar and lemon until soft, but still firm, approximately 8 minutes. Drain and set aside.

Preheat oven to 350°F.

Slice fennel and pears and layer alternately in four individual gratin dishes. Divide broth between dishes, season with salt and pepper and bake 15–20 minutes. Sprinkle with freshly grated Parmesan cheese and broil until golden brown. Garnish dish with fresh basil sprigs.

Serves 4.

Charlotte Lane Fennel and Pear Gratin ▶

GRILLED PORTOBELLO MUSHROOMS WITH MIXED PEPPERS AND CASSIS

ARBOR VIEW INN, LUNENBURG, NS

*Full of flavour, portobello mushrooms are large and meaty. They are found
in the produce section of larger supermarkets.*

4 large portobello mushrooms

4 fresh thyme sprigs

2–3 tablespoons extra virgin olive oil

1–2 tablespoons balsamic vinegar

coarse ground sea salt

pepper

2 large red bell pepper

2 large yellow bell pepper

1/2 cup extra virgin olive oil (2nd amount)

2–3 tablespoon balsamic vinegar (2nd amount)

coarsely ground pepper

coarse sea salt

1–2 tablespoons Cassis liqueur

Remove stems and clean mushrooms by brushing lightly. Divide each mushroom into 3 and arrange in a flat-bottomed baking dish. Gently tear the tender ends of the thyme and sprinkle over the mushrooms. Drizzle with olive oil and vinegar to lightly coat and season with salt and pepper. Let stand 1 hour, turn and let stand an additional hour.

Quarter peppers and remove core and seeds. Carefully shave the inner rind of the peppers so that you are left with a thin section of the outside skin.

Slice into a fine julienne. In a small bowl whisk together the olive oil (2nd amount) and vinegar (2nd amount). Stir in peppers, season with ground pepper and salt and marinate at least 1/2 hour.

Preheat grill to high setting. Grill mushrooms, turning until cooked, approximately 2 minutes per side.

Spoon pepper mixture into centre of plate and arrange mushrooms over peppers. Serve warm, garnished with additional thyme sprigs and a drizzle of Cassis.

Serves 4–6.

Grilled Portobello Mushrooms with Mixed Peppers and Cassis ▶

SPINACH CRÊPES WITH TOMATO COULIS

BLOMIDON INN, WOLFVILLE, NS

These tiny crêpes filled with a blend of spinach and cheese are a visual delight.

8–12 small crêpes

1/4 cup butter

1 small onion, coarsely chopped

1 bag fresh spinach, washed and stems removed, 10 ounce size

3/4 cup white wine

1/2 bulb oven roasted garlic*

salt and pepper

5 ounces cream cheese, softened

1/2 pound feta cheese crumbled

1 1/2 teaspoons fresh thyme, chopped

salt and pepper, to taste

3/4 to 1 cup fresh bread crumbs

Tomato Coulis, recipe follows

Roasted Roma Tomatoes, see recipe page 51

Prepare crêpes and set aside. In a medium skillet, melt butter and sweat onion for 5 minutes. Add spinach and cook until wilted. Deglaze pan with wine, add garlic and season with salt and pepper. Transfer spinach mixture to a food processor and purée. Add cream cheese and process until combined, then add feta and thyme and continue to process until smooth. Season with salt and pepper. Stir in enough bread crumbs to bind the stuffing together. Fill each crêpe with 2 tablespoons of mixture and roll.

Preheat oven to 350°F. To serve, warm crêpes in oven 10–15 minutes. Serve two crêpes on a pool of warm Tomato Coulis accompanied by Roasted Roma Tomatoes.

Serves 4–6.

* Oven Roasted Garlic: Lightly coat unpeeled garlic cloves with a little olive oil and bake until browned and softened, approximately 30 minutes. Gently squeeze garlic out of its peel with your fingers.

Tomato Coulis

5–6 Italian tomatoes, chopped
1 small onion, minced

2 cloves garlic, minced

2 tablespoons olive oil

3/4 cup white wine

2 tablespoons tomato paste

1 teaspoon fresh thyme, chopped

2–3 tablespoons heavy cream (35% m.f.) or to taste

salt and pepper, to taste

Sauté tomatoes, onion and garlic in hot oil until softened. Add wine, tomato paste, thyme and simmer until vegetables are cooked. Purée in a blender, return to heat and stir in cream. Season with salt and pepper.

Blomidon Inn's Spinach Crêpes with Tomato Coulis ▶

FENNEL CUSTARD WITH RATATOUILLE SLAW

INN ON THE LAKE, WAVERLEY, NS

Fresh fennel, available in most large supermarkets, has a broad bulbous base with pale green stems and wispy sprigs that resemble fresh dill. Chef Darrell MacMullin uses it to infuse a delicate flavour into the custard which he serves with Ratatouille Slaw.

1 1/2 tablespoons olive oil

1 tablespoon balsamic vinegar

salt and pepper, to taste

skin of 1 small eggplant, julienne

1 red bell pepper, julienne

1 yellow bell pepper, julienne

1 green bell pepper, julienne

skin of 1 small green zucchini, julienne

skin of 1 small yellow zucchini, julienne

Fennel Custard, recipe follows

Fresh fennel sprigs, as garnish

1 small tomato, seeded and julienne, as garnish

Using a wire whisk, combine oil and vinegar until emulsified. Season with salt and pepper.

In a small bowl, toss together eggplant, peppers and zucchini and drizzle with vinaigrette. Toss to coat.

To serve, place a small amount of the vegetables in the centre of four plates. Carefully remove custard from molds and place on top of slaw. Garnish with fresh fennel sprigs and julienne of tomato.

Fennel Custard

1 large bulb fennel

2 garlic cloves, minced

1 tablespoon olive oil

1 cup chicken stock

2 whole eggs

2 egg yolks

6 tablespoons heavy cream (35% m.f.)

1 tablespoon fennel seeds, roasted

Preheat oven to 350°F.

Finely chop fennel and mince garlic. Heat oil in a large pan and sauté fennel and garlic over medium heat 4–5 minutes, stirring constantly. Add stock and reduce to one half.

In a blender, combine whole eggs and egg yolks. With machine running, slowly pour in fennel mixture, cream, and seeds. Purée and strain.

Butter 4 small stainless-steel timbale molds and fill with custard. Bake in a water bath until firm, approximately 20 minutes. Chill.

Inn on the Lake's Fennel Custard and Ratatouille Slaw ▶

SOUP AND SALAD

*I*f you love fresh vegetables, you'll adore the varieties offered in this soup and salad section.

◄ *Elegantly presented Roasted Vegetable Soup with Pecan Quince Chutney*

ROASTED VEGETABLE SOUP WITH PECAN QUINCE CHUTNEY

THE WINDSOR HOUSE OF ST. ANDREWS, ST. ANDREWS, NB

Chef Patricia Bullock suggests preparing this soup a day in advance to allow the flavours to blend. The addition of the cream is optional and for the photo she added cream to half the soup. The Pecan Quince Chutney is not a true chutney, but is a wonderful accompaniment and simple to prepare.

2 pounds carrots

2 pounds parsnips

2 pounds turnips

2 pounds onions, chopped

2 bay leaves

1 teaspoon salt

1/2 teaspoon ground white pepper

1 cup heavy cream (35% m.f.), optional

Pecan Quince Chutney, recipe follows

Preheat oven to 350°F.

Peel carrots, parsnips, and turnips and cube. Place on a lightly greased baking sheet and roast until vegetables begin to turn golden brown, approximately 20–30 minutes.

Transfer roasted vegetables to a large kettle and add onion, bay leaves, salt, and pepper. Add enough water to the pot to cover the vegetables and bring to a boil. Simmer soup 1 hour. Remove bay leaves and purée, in batches, in a blender or food processor. Return purée to pot, adjust seasonings if necessary and stir in cream. Heat to serving temperature and serve topped with a tablespoon of Pecan Quince Chutney.

Serves 6

Pecan Quince Chutney

1/2 cup quince preserves

1/4 cup toasted pecan pieces, finely chopped

1 tablespoon finely diced red pepper

1/4 teaspoon cinnamon

dash of Tabasco sauce

Combine all ingredients and place a tablespoon in the centre of each soup bowl as garnish just before serving.

SPOT O'TEA HAM AND CAULIFLOWER CHOWDER

CATHERINE MCKINNON'S SPOT O'TEA RESTAURANT, STANLEY BRIDGE, PEI

Maritime cooks have been preparing chowders for years, and chef Harry Pineau's cauliflower and ham rendition is a favourite with patrons of Spot O'Tea Restaurant.

2 cups chopped cauliflower

2 cups diced potatoes

3/4 cup diced celery

1/2 cup diced onion

1 3/4 cups chicken stock

1/4 cup water

3 tablespoons butter, softened

2 tablespoons flour

1 cup heavy cream (35% m.f.)

1 1/2 cups milk

2 cups cubed cooked ham

fresh parsley, as garnish

In a large saucepan cook cauliflower, potatoes, celery, and onion in chicken stock and water until tender, about 10 minutes. Do not drain.

Knead together butter and flour, forming small balls. Stir cream and milk into chowder and add butter balls. Heat to a simmer and cook until slightly thickened. Add ham and continue simmering for an additional 10 minutes. Season to taste with salt and pepper. Serve garnished with fresh parsley.

Serves 6–8.

HARVEST GOLD SOUP

DUNCREIGAN COUNTRY INN, MABOU, NS

Eleanor Mullendore of Duncreigan Country Inn occasionally varies this recipe by adding 1/2 teaspoon curry or cumin to the soup. Be adventuresome and try all three versions.

1 medium onion, chopped

1 stalk celery, chopped

2 tablespoons butter

1 slice fresh ginger

1 large potato, peeled and diced

3 cups chicken stock

1/2 cup dry white wine

3 cups diced winter squash

1/2 cup heavy cream (35% m.f.)

salt and pepper, to taste

sour cream, as garnish

In a large saucepan, over medium heat, sauté onion and celery until tender, being careful not to brown. Add ginger slice, potato, and stock and simmer for 10 minutes. Add squash and continue to simmer until squash is tender. Remove ginger and purée soup in batches in a food processor. Reheat and stir in cream, taking care not to bring soup to a boil. Season with salt and pepper and serve with a dollop of sour cream.

Serves 4–6.

CURRIED POTATO SOUP WITH SALMON AND RED- OR OAK-LEAF LETTUCE

AMHERST SHORE COUNTRY INN, LORNEVILLE, NS

The chef at Amherst Shore Country Inn states that this is a very versatile recipe. A lighter version made without the salmon is an equally pleasing soup.

1/4 cup butter

1 1/2 cups Spanish onion, chopped medium fine

8 small potatoes, peeled and sliced 1/4-inch thick

2 cups rich chicken stock, preferably home made

1 1/2 teaspoons curry powder

2 cups heavy cream (35% m.f.)

salt and pepper, to taste

2 cups cooked salmon, flaked

3 ounces red-leaf or oak-leaf lettuce, rinsed, dried and sliced

In a large saucepan melt butter and sauté onions and potatoes for 3–4 minutes. Add chicken stock and 1 teaspoon curry, simmer until potatoes are cooked, approximately 15–20 minutes. Add cream and reheat just to a boil. Add more curry, if desired, and season with salt and pepper. Cool and refrigerate, covered for 24 hours.

To serve, add cooked salmon and reheat soup, then stir in lettuce.

Serves 6.

CREAM OF ZUCCHINI SOUP DUNDEE ARMS STYLE

DUNDEE ARMS, CHARLOTTETOWN, PEI

Chef Austin Clements serves this soup when prolific zucchini are at their best. Since zucchini grow as large as a baseball bat, it is difficult to determine medium-sized! I suggest you use approximately 3 cups of cubed zucchini for this recipe.

1 large onion, in medium dice

3 tablespoons clarified butter*

5 medium-sized zucchini, halved, seeded and in medium dice

6 cups chicken or vegetable stock

1 bay leaf

2 cups heavy cream (35% m.f.)

salt and pepper, to taste

fresh parsley, as garnish

Sauté onion in clarified butter until aromatic and translucent, approximately 5 minutes. Add zucchini and sauté 2 minutes, stirring occasionally. Stir in stock and bring to a boil. Add bay leaf, reduce heat and simmer until zucchini is soft, about 10–15 minutes. Remove bay leaf and purée soup in batches in a blender. Return purée to a simmer, stir in cream and season with salt and pepper. Serve garnished with fresh parsley.

Serves 6.

* To clarify butter: Slowly melt unsalted butter over very low heat. Do not stir. Remove from heat and skim the foam off the surface. Spoon remaining butter into a small bowl being careful to leave the milky sediment in the bottom of the pan.

Cream of Zucchini Soup Dundee Arms Style ▶

ABSOLUTELY THE BEST CARROT SOUP

JUBILEE COTTAGE COUNTRY INN, WALLACE, NS

Jubilee Cottage Country Inn has two small dining rooms where guests may be served dinner by advance reservations. This carrot soup is frequently on the menu.

2 tablespoons butter

4 cups thinly sliced carrots

1 large onion, chopped

3 tablespoons fresh ginger, chopped

3 cups chicken stock

1 cup orange juice

salt and pepper, to taste

1/4 cup heavy cream (35% m.f.)

zest from 1 orange, for garnish

fresh parsley or chives, for garnish

Melt butter in a heavy saucepan over low heat, stir in carrots, onion and ginger. Cover and cook 5 minutes. Stir in stock and bring to a boil. Reduce heat and simmer, covered, for 15 minutes. Remove from heat and cool slightly. Purée in batches in a food processor or blender. Return to saucepan and add orange juice, salt, pepper and heavy cream. Stir well and gently reheat, being careful not to bring to a boil.

Garnish with orange zest and chopped parsley or chives.

Serves 6.

FLORENTINE MANOR TOMATO SOUP

FLORENTINE MANOR HERITAGE INN, ALBERT, NB

Served at the Florentine Manor to rave reviews, this full-bodied soup is just the answer for a blustery winter day.

2 medium potatoes, peeled and diced

1 small onion, diced

4 cups water

1/2 teaspoon salt

1 2/3 cups stewed tomatoes, crushed

1/3 teaspoon baking soda

2 tablespoons butter

3 tablespoons sugar

salt and pepper, to taste

1 rounded tablespoon flour

1/2 cup cold water

grated Cheddar cheese, as garnish

In a large saucepan, bring potatoes, onion, water, and salt to a boil. Immediately lower heat and simmer until vegetables are tender, approximately 20 minutes. Stir in crushed tomatoes and return to a boil. Add soda and skim off foam. Stir in butter, sugar and season with salt and pepper. Thicken soup by stirring together the flour and water, then whisk into soup and return to serving temperature.

Garnish each bowl with a generous grating of Cheddar cheese.

Serves 4.

YELLOW SQUASH AND SHRIMP BISQUE

CANDLERIGGS DINING ROOM, INDIAN HARBOUR, NS

Squash and Shrimp Bisque is a popular choice at Candleriggs and to quote owner Jean Cochrane, "It is sooo ... good!"

1 pound winter squash, peeled and cubed

4 cups chicken broth

2 cups water

6 tablespoons butter

1/3 cup flour

1/3 cup onion, finely chopped

1/3 cup green pepper, finely chopped

1/3 cup celery, finely chopped

1/4 teaspoon white pepper

2 bay leaves

1/8–1/4 teaspoon cayenne pepper

1/2 teaspoon powdered thyme

1/2 teaspoon salt

1/2 pound raw shrimp, peeled, deveined and roughly chopped

1/2 cup heavy cream (35% m.f.)

In a medium saucepan, simmer squash in broth and water until tender, approximately 20 minutes. Drain squash, reserving liquid, purée and set aside.

Melt butter in a large saucepan and stir in flour. Whisk roux over medium heat until golden, approximately 6 minutes. Add onion, bell pepper and celery and cook 5 minutes. Stir in puréed squash, reserved liquid, white pepper, bay leaves, cayenne, thyme, and salt. Simmer 20 minutes, add shrimp and cream. Return to a simmer and cook an additional 6 minutes. Remove bay leaves.

Serves 6

SPRING ASPARAGUS SOUP WITH MALPEQUE OYSTERS

SEASONS IN THYME, SUMMERSIDE, PEI

The arrival of asparagus in the spring brings the promise of good things to come! At Seasons in Thyme, owner-chef Stefan Czapalay marries the tender asparagus with Malpeque oysters in this delightful soup.

2 small leeks, white part only

1 tablespoon olive oil

4 cups vegetable or chicken stock

1 medium potato, peeled and diced

1 pound asparagus, ends trimmed

12 Malpeque oysters in the shell

2 tablespoons heavy cream (35% m.f.)

salt and freshly ground pepper, to taste

fresh chervil or parsley, as garnish

Carefully trim tops from leeks and rinse thoroughly. Heat oil in a saucepan over medium heat and sauté leeks until softened but not browned, approximately 8 minutes. Stir in stock and potato, bring to a boil then reduce heat and simmer 10 minutes.

While stock is simmering, clean and trim each asparagus spear into 4 or 5 pieces, add to soup and continue to simmer until vegetables are tender.

Shuck oysters. Strain juice to remove bits of shell or sand. Divide oysters and juice among four soup bowls.

Purée soup in batches in a blender until smooth. Return purée to saucepan and bring to a boil. Stir in cream and season with salt and pepper. Ladle soup over oysters and garnish with chopped chervil or parsley sprigs.

Serves 4.

Spring Asparagus Soup with Malpeque Oysters as served at Seasons in Thyme Restaurant ▶

PUMPKIN SEED SALAD

FLORENTINE MANOR HERITAGE INN, ALBERT, NB

Innkeeper Mary Tingley suggests washing, drying, and chilling the salad greens at least two hours before serving.

1 head iceberg lettuce

1 head red leaf lettuce

2 tomatoes, in wedges

1/2 English style cucumber, sliced

2 stalks celery, sliced

1/4 pound fresh mushrooms, cleaned and sliced

1/2 cup raw baby pumpkin seeds, cleaned

grated Cheddar cheese, as garnish

Garlic Vinaigrette, recipe follows

Prepare salad greens and keep chilled in the refrigerator. Divide greens between four salad plates. Top with tomato wedges, cucumber, celery, and mushroom slices.

Slice open a baby pumpkin; remove and rinse small seeds. Sprinkle generously with fresh pumpkin seeds and garnish with grated Cheddar and a drizzle of Garlic Vinaigrette.

Serves 4.

Garlic Vinaigrette

1/2 cup vegetable oil

1/4 cup cider vinegar

2 cloves garlic, minced

1/4 teaspoon each salt, pepper, basil and sugar

In an electric blender or food processor, combine all ingredients until emulsified. Yields 3/4 cup dressing.

Florentine Manor's Pumpkin Seed Salad ▶

SPINACH SALAD WITH COTTAGE DILL DRESSING

THE INNLET CAFÉ, MAHONE BAY, NS

Fresh spinach is an excellent choice as a salad green. At the Innlet Café owner-chef Jack Sorenson uses the expiry date on the cottage cheese container as a guide to how long this delightful dressing can be stored.

12-ounce package fresh spinach

1/2 cup carrot thinly sliced

2 stalks celery, sliced

8 radishes, sliced

2 eggs, hard boiled and cut in wedges

1/2 cup alfalfa sprouts

1/2 cup grated Swiss cheese

1/4 cup toasted sunflower seeds

Cottage Dill Dressing, recipe follows

Wash and dry spinach, and remove large stems. Tear into bite-sized pieces. Place spinach, carrot, celery, radish, and eggs in a large salad bowl, drizzle with dressing and toss lightly. Divide between 4 salad plates.

Top each salad with alfalfa sprouts, Swiss cheese and sunflower seeds.

Serves 4.

Cottage Dill Dressing

1 cup cottage cheese

1 cup egg-based mayonnaise

2 tablespoons vegetable oil

1/4 cup lemon juice

1 large garlic clove, mashed

2 teaspoons dried dill weed

1/4 teaspoon salt

generous grindings of pepper

1/4 cup whole milk (3 1/2% m.f.)

Using an electric mixer, combine all ingredients. Store any unused dressing refrigerated in a covered container. Yields 2 cups.

BROCCOLI SALAD

THE MURRAY MANOR BED AND
BREAKFAST, YARMOUTH, NS

*Broccoli is an excellent vegetable to serve as a side
salad. Its bright green colour and crisp texture
complement a variety of other ingredients.*

1 large bunch fresh broccoli

1/2 cup sultana raisins

1/2 cup sunflower seeds or chopped walnuts

2 tablespoons candied ginger, finely diced

1/2 cup mayonnaise

salt and pepper, to taste

Cut broccoli into bite-sized flowerettes and
blanch in boiling, salted water for 2 minutes.
Immediately drain broccoli and rinse with ice
water to stop the cooking process.

Combine broccoli, raisins, sunflower seeds,
and ginger in a bowl. Toss with mayonnaise
and season with salt and pepper. Serve chilled.

Serves 4.

MURRAY MANOR POLISH ONIONS

THE MURRAY MANOR BED AND
BREAKFAST, YARMOUTH, NS

*This recipe is for the busy cook who appreciates a
dish that may be prepared in advance. Similar to
the cucumber salads made famous on Nova
Scotia's South Shore, Polish Onions is delicious
and easy to prepare.*

1/2 cup water

1/2 cup vinegar

1/3 cup sugar

1 teaspoon salt

1 large Spanish onion, thinly sliced

1 cup sour cream

celery seed and freshly ground pepper, as
garnish

In a deep bowl, stir until dissolved the water,
vinegar, sugar, and salt. Place onions in a bowl
and cover with vinegar solution. Refrigerate
8 hours.

At serving time drain onion and toss with sour
cream. Garnish with a sprinkling of celery
seeds and freshly ground pepper.

Serves 4.

SNOW-PEA AND POTATO SALAD WITH MINT-PESTO DRESSING

GOWRIE HOUSE COUNTRY INN, SYDNEY MINES, NS

Innkeeper Clifford Matthews loves to garden almost as much as he loves to cook! He has a ready supply of fresh mint in the inn's gardens for preparing his tasty mint-pesto dressing.

1/2 pound snow peas, trimmed

2 pounds baby new potatoes, scrubbed

1/4 cup fresh chives, snipped

1/2 cup loosely packed fresh mint leaves

1/4 cup olive oil

2 tablespoons toasted pine nuts

2 tablespoons freshly grated Parmesan cheese

black pepper

additional snipped chives, as garnish

Submerge snow peas in a large saucepan of boiling salted water for 2–3 minutes, or until just tender. Remove with a slotted spoon and refresh under cold running water. Drain well and set aside.

Cook potatoes in the same saucepan for 15–20 minutes or until tender. Drain well, then return potatoes to the saucepan over low heat for a minute to dry. Remove from heat and cool.

Prepare pesto by combining chives, mint, oil, pine nuts, and Parmesan cheese in food processor until fairly smooth. Season with pepper, to taste.

Place potatoes and snow peas in a large salad bowl, drizzle with pesto and toss gently. Garnish with chives.

Serves 4–6.

MAKE-AHEAD DISHES

*E*very clever cook has some make-ahead recipes on file. Your guests will appreciate your good planning

◄ *Baked Broccoli Casserole from the Ledges Inn*

BAKED BROCCOLI CASSEROLE

THE LEDGES INN, DOAKTOWN, NB

Innkeeper Caroline St. Pierre enjoys having a dish or two prepared in advance of dinner. This Baked Broccoli Casserole lends itself well to early preparation and may accompany the main dish in the oven.

2 bunches fresh broccoli, trimmed

3 tablespoons butter

3 tablespoons flour

1/2 cup chicken stock

1 cups milk

1 cup grated old white Cheddar cheese

15 ritz crackers, in crumbs

Preheat oven to 350°F.

Separate broccoli into flowerettes and blanch in boiling, salted water for 4 minutes. Drain and rinse in ice water to stop cooking process. Thoroughly drain and place in a lightly greased casserole.

Melt butter in a saucepan and whisk in flour, stirring constantly for 2 minutes. Carefully whisk in stock and milk and simmer 5 minutes. Add grated cheese and stir until melted.

Pour sauce over broccoli and sprinkle casserole with cracker crumbs. Bake until bubbly and broccoli is tender approximately 30 minutes.

Serves 6–8.

CREAMY CARROTS AND PARSNIPS

THE WHITMAN INN, KEMPT, NS

This is a busy cooks "dream recipe"! Easy to prepare, it can be popped in the oven at a minute's notice.

4 cups sliced carrots

2 cups sliced parsnip

1 medium leek, white part only, cleaned and chopped

1 cup mayonnaise

2 tablespoons chopped parsley

2 tablespoons prepared horseradish

1/4 teaspoon salt

1/8 teaspoon pepper

1 cup cracker crumbs

2 tablespoons butter, melted

In a large saucepan cover carrots, parsnip, and leek with water and bring to a boil. Reduce heat and simmer until vegetables are crisp tender. Drain and place in a large bowl.

Preheat oven to 350°F.

In a separate bowl whisk together the mayonnaise, parsley, horseradish, salt and pepper. Toss mixture with vegetables and transfer to a greased oven-proof baking dish, sprinkle with cracker crumbs and drizzle with butter. Bake until bubbly and browned, approximately 25 minutes.

Serves 6.

Creamy Carrots & Parsnips ▶

VEGETABLE LASAGNE WITH LEMON-THYME VEGETABLE BROTH

INN ON THE LAKE, WAVERLEY, NS

A medley of summer vegetables, all picked at their peak inspired chef Mark Baillie to assemble this lasagne-style dish.

2 tablespoons butter

1 large Yukon gold potato, sliced lengthwise into thin strips

salt and pepper, to season

1/2 cup grated Parmesan cheese

2 red bell peppers, roasted (see page 60)

2 yellow bell peppers, roasted

1 yellow zucchini, sliced lengthwise

1 green zucchini, sliced lengthwise

6 cooked artichoke hearts, sliced

2 tablespoons butter, second amount

Lemon-Thyme Vegetable Broth, recipe follows

Preheat oven to 350°F. Line a straight sided baking pan with foil and grease with butter.

Using 1/3 of the potato, cover the bottom of the pan with a single layer, overlapping slightly. Season with salt and pepper and sprinkle with 1/3 of the Parmesan cheese.

Slice prepared peppers into thin slices and place a layer of red pepper on top of the potatoes. Add a layer of yellow zucchini, green zucchini, artichokes and yellow pepper.

Repeat with layers of vegetables ending with a layer of potato. Cover with foil and place a weight on top of pan to hold vegetables in place.

Bake 2 hours, remove from oven and let cool with weight still on top of vegetables. Remove from pan and cut into 4 equal squares.

To serve, sauté lasagne squares in butter until golden brown. Place squares in shallow bowls and surround with a spoonful of Vegetable Broth. Garnish with a sprig of fresh lemon thyme.

Serves 4.

Lemon-Thyme Vegetable Broth

3 cups vegetable broth

1 1/2 leeks, cleaned and chopped

1 Spanish onions, chopped

2 stalks celery

1 parsnip, peeled and chopped

1 small turnip, chopped

1/2 tablespoon whole black peppercorns

2 bay leaves

1 whole clove

2 sprigs lemon thyme

zest of 1/3 lemon

Combine broth, vegetables, and spices in a large stock pot. Bring to a boil, reduce heat and simmer 1 hour. Strain and add 2 sprigs fresh lemon thyme and lemon zest. Reduce to 2 cups.

Vegetable Lasagne with Lemon-Thyme Vegetable Broth ▶

RATATOUILLE

BLOMIDON INN, WOLFVILLE, NS

*The gardens of Blomidon Inn supply the chefs with an abundance of summer vegetables.
This ratatouille, served to rave reviews, is best prepared when tomatoes are at their peak
and zucchini threaten to take over the vegetable plot!*

2 tablespoons olive oil

1 small onion, chopped

1 cup chopped bell peppers, red, green or yellow

2 cloves garlic, minced

1 small zucchini, chopped

1/2 medium eggplant, diced

3 large tomatoes

1/2 – 1/3 cup tomato juice

1 tablespoon balsamic vinegar

1 tablespoon fresh basil, chopped, or
1/2 tablespoon dried

1 teaspoon fresh oregano, chopped, or
1/2 teaspoon dried

1 teaspoon fresh thyme, chopped or
1/2 teaspoon dried

1 tablespoon tomato paste

salt and pepper, to taste

In a large saucepan, sauté onion, peppers, and garlic in hot oil, stirring frequently. Add zucchini, eggplant, and tomatoes and sauté until all vegetables are tender. Stir in tomato juice, vinegar, and herbs. Bring to a boil and stir in tomato paste. Simmer until sauce has thickened. Season with salt and pepper and serve in individual *au gratin* dishes.

Serves 4–6.

Summer Vegetables at their best as served in Blomidon Inn's Ratatouille ▶

ENTRÉE ACCOMPANIMENTS

*M*ore, much more than

some vegetables on the side, these creations will be

partners, rather than accompanists to your entrée dishes.

◄ *Green Beans Topped with Pecans and Honey from Little Shemogue Country Inn*

GREEN BEANS TOPPED WITH PECANS AND HONEY

LITTLE SHEMOGUE COUNTRY INN, PORT ELGIN, NB

Crisp, garden-fresh green beans provide a colourful addition to many dishes. For the photo presentation, chef Petra Sudbrack served her beans as an accompaniment for roasted pork tenderloins.

1 pound fresh green beans

1/2 cup butter

4 roasted cloves of garlic*

2 tablespoons liquid honey

1 cup broken pecans

Rinse green beans and remove stems. In a medium saucepan, bring beans to a boil in lightly salted water, reduce heat and simmer until crisp tender, approximately 10 minutes. Drain.

While beans are cooking, melt butter in a small skillet. Squeeze roasted garlic cloves into butter and sauté 2 minutes. Stir in honey and cook an additional 2 minutes. Stir in broken pecans and keep warm.

To serve, place a small amount of glazed pecans on top of warm beans.

Serves 4.

* To Oven Roast Garlic: See recipe page 18

WICKED WHIPPED SQUASH

FALCOURT INN, NICTAUX, NS

There is no way of telling if a squash is going to be "wet" or "dry" when cooked. At Falcourt Inn Chef Kelvin Boutilier uses dehydrated potato flakes to thicken his squash if the cooked results are too wet.

1 cup cooked buttercup squash

1 cup cooked acorn squash

1 cup cooked spaghetti squash

1 cup cooked potato

1/4 cup brown sugar

1/4 cup butter

2–4 tablespoons dehydrated potato flakes, optional

1 teaspoon salt

1/2 teaspoon white pepper

Drain cooked squash and cooked potato in a colander and let stand 5 minutes to air dry. Combine vegetables with brown sugar and butter in a mixing bowl and whip on medium speed until smooth. If mixture is too wet, sprinkle with potato flakes, a little at a time and process on low speed until desired consistency. Season with salt and pepper.

Serves 4–6.

TOMATOES STUFFED WITH ROASTED SQUASH

MARSHLANDS INN, SACKVILLE, NB

Chef Jeffrey Ayres of Marshlands Inn fills vine-ripened tomatoes with roasted squash, a perfect accompaniment to baked chicken or pork entrées.

8 medium tomatoes

1 small butternut squash

1 tablespoon dried rosemary

1/2 cup brown sugar

1 teaspoon curry powder

1/2 teaspoon ground cumin

salt and pepper, to taste

Cut a small piece off the bottom of each tomato so that they stand firmly. Remove core from tomatoes from the top so that they form a cup. Place tomatoes upside down on paper towels to drain.

Preheat oven to 400°F.

Peel and dice squash into very small cubes, rinse and reserve seeds. Toss squash with rosemary, sugar, curry, cumin, salt, and pepper and bake on a sheet until soft, approximately 20 minutes.

In a separate roasting pan, bake squash seeds until golden brown. Remove and set aside.

To serve, fill tomatoes with squash mixture and return to oven for 5 minutes. Serve garnished with squash seeds.

Serves 8.

ROASTED ROMA TOMATOES

BLOMIDON INN, WOLFVILLE, NS

Summertime flavour at its best: chef Sean Laceby marinates then roasts his Italian tomatoes to perfection!

10–12 Italian-style tomatoes, cut in wedges

3 large cloves garlic, puréed

2 teaspoons fresh thyme, chopped

1 tablespoon fresh basil, chopped

2 teaspoons fresh oregano, chopped

3 tablespoons balsamic vinegar

2 tablespoons olive oil

salt and pepper, to taste

In a large bowl combine all ingredients and let stand 1 hour. Preheat oven to 250°F. Drain tomatoes and place on a baking sheet. Roast 3 hours.

BEETS DIJONNAISE

HALLIBURTON HOUSE INN,
HALIFAX, NS

The chef says this is guaranteed to make beet lovers out of the most jaded palate. Try it and you'll agree with his prediction.

1/2 cup heavy cream (35% m.f.)

1 heaping teaspoon Dijon-style mustard

2 cups cooked beets

Mix cream and mustard, until well blended, in a medium-sized saucepan. Add beets, sliced or halved. Simmer until cream is reduced and sauce has thickened and clings to the beets, approximately 8 minutes. Serve immediately.

Serves 4.

BABY BEETS WITH GOLDEN PINEAPPLE SAUCE

AMHERST SHORE COUNTRY INN,
LORNEVILLE, NS

The extensive gardens at the Amherst Shore Country Inn ensures a supply of fresh baby beets. Innkeeper Donna Laceby is innovative in her preparation, enhancing the flavours with the addition of fresh pineapple.

1/2 cup pineapple or apple juice

1/4 cup brown sugar

1 tablespoon cornstarch

1 teaspoon lemon juice

1 tablespoon butter

1 cup fresh golden pineapple, cut into chunks

4 cups cooked baby beets, whole or halved

In a medium saucepan combine juice, sugar, and cornstarch. Bring to a boil, reduce heat, and simmer until thickened. Stir in lemon juice, butter, pineapple, and beets; return to serving temperature.

Serves 6.

Amherst Shore Inn's Baby Beets with Golden Pineapple Sauce ▶

CARROTS WITH GRAND MARNIER AND FRESH CILANTRO

AMHERST SHORE COUNTRY INN, LORNEVILLE, NS

These are not your average carrots! Cooked until barely crisp tender, this dish provides a taste sensation.

2 cups fresh carrots, in sticks or sliced diagonally

1 tablespoon butter

1 teaspoon sugar

1 tablespoon Grand Marnier liqueur

1 teaspoon finely grated orange zest

1 tablespoon fresh cilantro, chopped, as garnish

Pare and cut carrots into preferred shape and cook until crisp tender.

In a small saucepan melt butter, stir in sugar, Grand Marnier and zest. Pour over drained carrots and stir to coat evenly. Serve warm sprinkled with chopped cilantro.

Serves 4–6.

MARSHLANDS INN'S STUFFED RED PEPPERS

MARSHLANDS INN, SACKVILLE, NB

Chef Jeffrey Ayres of Marshlands Inn serves this colourful dish when summer vegetables are at their peak.

4 red bell peppers

1 leek, white part only

1 cup oil-packed sun-dried tomatoes, drained

1 pound mushrooms, sliced

2 tablespoons olive oil

1/4 cup vodka

1 cup heavy cream (35% m.f.)

1/2 cup feta cheese, crumbled

1 cup corn kernels

1/4 cup grated Parmesan cheese

salt and pepper, to taste

Preheat oven to 400°F.

Core peppers to form a cup and set aside. Clean leek and slice in julienne strips. Thinly slice sun-dried tomatoes. Heat olive oil in a skillet and sauté leeks, tomatoes, and mushrooms for 1 minute. Add vodka, cream, crumbled cheese, corn, and grated Parmesan cheese. Season to taste with salt and pepper and spoon into pepper shells. Bake 4–5 minutes.

Serves 4.

Marshlands Inn's Stuffed Red Peppers ▶

THE LAST WORD IN LATKES

JUBILEE COTTAGE COUNTRY INN,
WALLACE, NS

3 large baking potatoes, peeled and grated

1 large onion, grated

1 egg, beaten

salt and pepper to taste

2 tablespoons flour

1/2 teaspoon baking powder

vegetable oil for frying

For best results grate potatoes into very cold water, then drain and squeeze out all excess liquid. Drain liquid from onion. In a large bowl mix together the potato, onion, egg, salt, pepper, flour, and baking powder.

Heat a film of oil in a large heavy non-stick skillet over medium high heat. Drop two heaping tablespoons of potato mixture into the skillet and flatten with a spoon. Fry until golden brown, approximately 4 minutes per side. Drain on paper towel and keep warm.

Yields 12 latkes.

NEW NEW BRUNSWICK POTATOES WITH GREEN BEANS

SHADOW LAWN COUNTRY INN,
ROTHESAY, NB

This dish calls for the tiniest potatoes available. Tapenade is a thick paste of ground black olives, capers, and olive oil and is found in the speciality food section of grocery stores. For the photo presentation chef Glen White served his potatoes with baby spring lamb.

1 pound tiny new potatoes

1/2 pound green beans, ends removed

1/4 cup pine nuts, toasted

1/2 cup plum tomatoes, in large dice

1/4 cup black olives, pitted and sliced

2 tablespoons black olive tapenade

2 tablespoons mayonnaise

salt and pepper, to taste

1/4 cup feta cheese, crumbled

Cook potatoes in boiling salted water until barely fork tender. Drain, set aside and keep warm.

Blanch beans in boiling water for 4 minutes, drain and keep warm.

To serve, toss potatoes and beans with pine nuts, tomatoes, and black olives.

In a small bowl, whisk together tapenade and mayonnaise, add to vegetables and toss to coat. Season with salt and pepper and serve sprinkled with crumbled feta.

Serves 4.

New New Brunswick Potatoes with Green Beans ▶

ROASTED VEGETABLE NAPOLEONS

THE WHITMAN INN, KEMPT, NS

Prepare these elegant napoleons early in the day and finish off in the oven just before serving time. At the inn, the chef occasionally adds a little grated Cheddar or Mozzarella cheese to the cream cheese for added flavour.

6 slices of a medium potato

6 slices tomato

6 slices zucchini

6 slices eggplant

1 whole portobello mushroom

1/4 cup olive oil

freshly ground black pepper

1 red pepper, roasted*, as garnish

8 ounces cream cheese, softened

3 cloves garlic minced

1–2 tablespoons fresh chives, minced

1/2 teaspoon thyme

salt and pepper, to taste

Preheat oven to 400°F. Lightly brush both sides of the potatoes, tomato, zucchini, eggplant, and mushroom with olive oil and sprinkle with pepper. Roast on a greased baking sheet until just tender, allowing 10 minutes for the potato and 5 minutes for the remainder of the vegetables. Cool. Slice mushroom into strips.

Prepare roasted red pepper and cut in julienne strips.

In a bowl combine cheese, garlic, chives, and thyme.

At serving time, preheat oven to 400°F.

Layer potato, tomato, zucchini and eggplant slices with 1 teaspoon of cheese mixture between each vegetable. Top with mushroom and roasted pepper strips. Season with salt and pepper and bake until heated through and cheese starts to melt, approximately 6–10 minutes.

Serves 6.

* To roast bell peppers: Grill pepper until it is burnt black on all sides. Immediately place in a brown paper bag until cooled. Peel blackened skin from pepper, remove stalk and inner seeds and slice.

CINNAMON-SCENTED BUTTERNUT SQUASH RISOTTO

SHADOW LAWN COUNTRY INN, ROTHESAY, NB

Italian-style short-grained arborio rice must be cooked by adding the warm stock gradually, in small batches. The results are well worth the effort.

2 cups arborio rice

4 cups hot chicken stock

1/2 cup white wine

2 tablespoons vegetable oil

1 butternut squash, peeled and cut into 1/4-inch cubes

1 tablespoon cinnamon

2 tablespoons fresh herbs, chopped (rosemary, thyme, parsley etc.)

2 tablespoons butter

1/4 cup Parmesan cheese

Cook rice following package directions using stock and wine. Set aside and keep warm. Heat oil over medium heat and sauté squash cubes until tender. Dust squash with cinnamon. Fold squash into cooked rice, toss with herbs, butter and Parmesan cheese.

Serves 4.

SEASONS IN THYME'S ROSEMARY-ROASTED CAULIFLOWER

SEASONS IN THYME, SUMMERSIDE, PEI

Seasons in Thyme's chef Stefan Czapalay grows many of his herbs in the garden adjacent to the restaurant. In this dish he combines fresh rosemary with cauliflower and suggests serving the dish with roasted meat entrées.

1 small head cauliflower

2 tablespoons extra virgin olive oil

1 1/2 tablespoon chopped fresh rosemary

salt and pepper, to taste

1 tablespoon butter

Preheat oven to 450°F. Rinse cauliflower and break into bite-sized pieces and place in a large bowl. Sprinkle with oil and toss until cauliflower is completely coated. Sprinkle with rosemary and season with salt and pepper, toss again to coat.

Place cauliflower in an *au gratin* dish. Dot top of vegetables with butter. Bake 15 minutes or until cauliflower is tender.

Serves 4.

An elegant presentation of Seasons in Thyme's Rosemary Roasted Cauliflower ▶